Spiral Bound

# Spiral Bound

an anthology of poetry and songs
published as a part of the *Gene Genie* exhibition

Hearing Eye

Hearing Eye
Torriano Poetry Pamphlet Series No.30
Published Summer 2000
ISBN 1 870841 65 4

Some poems have previously appeared in the following publications
*Chimaeras - their origins* from *Chimaeras*, Hearing Eye, 1994;
*Magic Roundabout* and *Mitosis* from
*Fairground of Madness*, Rockingham Press, 1992
*Perseus in Retrospect, Dear Dawkins...* and *Now I Know*
from David Kuhrt, *In Emphasis on Facts*, 1996
*Of Weaning and Desire* first published in *Staple* 45, 1999
*Brecht* in *Acumen* Spring 2000
*The Law of Natural Selection* from *The New Czech Poetry*, Bloodaxe Books 1988

The following are set to music: *Designer Kidz* and *Food'n Health'n Hope*
(available on CD from PO Box 23, High Street, Glastonbury, BA6 9DP);
and *There's something in the air*

This publication has been made possible with financial assistance from the
London Arts Board.

**Spiral Bound has been produced to accompany
Gene Genie: Making Choices About Genetic Engineering
an art/science exhibition**

printed by Catford Print Centre

# Introduction

We don't know what the first poem in the world spoke of, but one of the earliest pictures in human history is of the antlered man in the cave of Les Trois Freres, France.

The image of a merging of species for reasons of magic, metaphor or myth has been universal in human culture, but now with technological changes the old pictures have a new cast to them. The Minotaur, Anansi the Spider Man, and Ganesh have all gained an additional meaning now that metaphor is being replaced with the literal.

We weren't born yesterday, and many millions of people have spent many thousands of years trying to understand the nature of life, of who we are biologically and how we as one species relate to the plants, animals and environments around us. We have inherited this mass of knowledge in a form called 'culture', much of it in the language of poetry, stories and pictures.

Unless we are going to start from the cave again it is important that the thoughts of poets and artists feed into the debate on genetic engineering. As David Kuhrt says in 'The Sixth Episode'

> The earth is an accumulator of cryptic intelligence,
> and you and I are the heart. We know the score.
> Examine the in-put: with peripheral eyes I am, and am
> being seen. I see into, not out of the globe. I act,
> and do not identify the cause

Moreover if we are ever going to get to a position of democratic decision-making about the applications of scientific technologies in our society we need to assert the value of these other languages in the discussion.

This collection covers a broad span of writing, from a poet's vision of a biological process (*Mitosis*), to protest songs such as *Designer Kidz* and *Food n' Health n' Hope*. These visions are the equivalent of text book diagrams, they are images that we need to think through and to understand with.

Poetry can add another dimension of subtlety to the simple line drawings we are offered as an explanation of biological life.

*Emily Johns*

# Chimaeras - Their Origins

Celestial Sophia sat enthroned
Within the darkness of the Unknown God.
It was the Sixth Day, and she was busy
Sewing and snipping, and cutting out patterns –
Patterns of quadrupeds, beasts and cattle,
Serpents, alligators, human beings.
The selfish genes, her servants,
And the environmental factors
Stood by to work those patterns out.
But there were remnants which they rejected –
Heads and tails, wings and limbs and claws.
They drifted into the trashcan of the Cosmos.

Beelzebub, Lucifer and their confederates
The Rebel Angels had all been swept there
Some days previously. The babyish devils
Delighted in those anonymous fragments,
Creating chimaeras, beasts discordantly made up
Of incompatible parts – as hippogriffs,
Sphinxes, bucentaurs, tragopans,
Gorgons and cockatrices.
But the devils soon matured
And got engrossed in a more adult project –
The engineering of the Fall of Man.

Discarded now, the chimaeras
Still bombinated in their vacuum.

John Heath-Stubbs

# Mitosis*

On the ramparts, chromosome soldiers wake
and twist like hands at a funeral.
Woodsmoke drifts in from the fields,
builds a mirror.
See – it borrows your face
your lavender eyes
the bottle-green dress you always wore,
the tick of your watch.
Doppelganger.
Stalking you like a grizzly bear
your shoulders turned to snow.

Out of the mist – a general
sorts pairs from the jumble:
you this pole                    your double that
east                                west.
In the thimble of distance
between perfect left      and perfect right
he draws a wall
delicate as grief.

One slip and the cancer begins.

*Danielle Hope*

*The act of a cell exactly reproducing itself to grow.

10

# Fruit

They fled without much baggage – clothes they'd made
from leaves, all-purpose blankets from the skins
of sacrificial sheep. They knew the sin
of nakedness, God knows, and were afraid
it might be – cold? – out there. How beautiful
the world they left behind! They looked around
and half in shadow saw a ripened mound
of fruit beneath *that tree*. (Might as well
be killed for wolves as lambs.) Imagination
breeds anxiety. Lucky they were
to be alive, after the fall. So far,
so good. But travel requires preparation.
Eve piled high the fruit of Wisdom's tree
in a basket woven hurriedly.

Bewildering, the land beyond the gates,
so unlike Eden. People living there
as if forever! Stealthily...aware
instinctively suspicion fell on late
arrivals...Adam waited as Eve searched
the faces. Maybe...Cain?...Their skins were different,
lighter from less sunlight; eyes observant,
wary; tighter lips. As Cain was cursed,
were they? How sensible of Eve to pack
a lunch. No need to beg. Not yet. He shuddered
at a sudden wind, then heard the thunder
blasting from the sky, saw heaven black
as rage reflected in an inner change.
Eve noticed Adam coming over strange.

Not only evil/good, but something grey –
of many shades of grey – between them stood.
All on their own they must begin to put
things right, for God had turned his face away,
and everything was surely wrong, askew.
The earth no longer flat nor still, it twirled
around the sun, was one of many worlds;
the stars not simply lights; the sun and moon,
mere accidents of nature; heaven not up
above at all, but all around, and man emerged,
not from the hand of God, but, more absurd,
anomalously from some thumbless ape.
They burned their dead, left nothing to the vultures.
Eve set about inventing agriculture.

The earth felt warm and loving to their hands –
turning the soil, filling it with seed,
like lovers answering each other's need.
As goats and sheep and oxen crossed the land
their precious droppings fertilised the loam.
It seemed a kind of magic, how the pieces
of the world all came together, species
helping species. Adam named it 'home'.
All by themselves they'd made it, without God
(who turned away), another Eden in
this land which they had ploughed and seeded
and *improved* – such glory from plain sod!
The stolen fruit of Wisdom reproduced
new strains of sweeter, unforbidden fruit.

Eve gave this finer fruit to Adam, now
grown restless. He had learnt to hunt and fish
and sport with wolves: How had he come to this,
to be a common drudge behind a plough?
At night, alone – for now the nights were long
(a bride no more, Eve had become a wife) –
he keened his mind and his old hunting knife,
and dreamed of forests where a man still strong
could prove against a stronger enemy
true might lay in the power to invent.
Did God not say man should be dominant?
'Sweat of the brow'? What did that mean, but he
must furrow not the soil but his great brain
to render the whole world as his domain?

Slaughtering domestic animals
dismayed his appetite...in this, quite like
their Cain. He had Cain's temper, and could strike:
Eve watched her words, tended the vegetables.
One day he'd leave her for the hunt , she thought.
'Fair game,' he called it. (Often the kill was far
from edible.) He hung his trophies in the barn.
Eve wouldn't have them in the house. They fought
about this, but she had her way. He honed
his flints, turned ploughshares into swords. Well,
years went by – millennia – until
the barn became an arsenal and bones
of fairer game – human bones – burst through
the walls. Time for her to go, Eve knew.

She packed her bags with seeds she had not sown,
and took what she might need for yet another
journey. Her third son begged to go with her.
She hugged Seth fiercely, promised she would phone...
One secret, sacred fruit she would not share
with anyone. Its seed had fallen out
(whether good or evil lay in doubt):
To her experienced eye, unique. A pair
of twisted, stringy shapes – a double helix? –
looked like the beginning of the end.
She'd squandered Knowledge; nor did she defend
her Wisdom. This last prize... she *must* conceal it.
Key-like, she hung it on her chatelaine.
Adam found her wandering in the rain.

He had his knives now and his slaves and all
those wonderful machines for blowing up
the world, but nothing ever is enough
for some. He kept remembering the Fall,
the garden disappearing in the fog,
Eve's little hand in his, her frightened face,
how Abel died, Cain's exile in disgrace,
and worst, the awful, angry eyes of God,
who turned away. He cried out for revenge.
From Eve's dead palm, the mystifying stone
unraveled magic powers in his own,
alive with greed – and grief. That life should hinge
on this! Oh, bitter alchemy! *Stillborn,
the gilded pear, the jaded husks of corn,*

*and none, save God, to mourn.*

*Leah Fritz*

14

# The Law of Natural Selection

The Balt-Orient Express which starts in Berlin
is already ninety minutes late on arrival in Prague
The engine driver's in no hurry to get anywhere
The engine driver is not getting married tomorrow
Unlike me

Some people have a lucky hand
in anything they do
My father was one of them
The horses in Chuchle
ran to his hopes
Fish swam to his hook
as if drugged
Mushrooms grew before his eyes
He always drew the right card in the end
And mother was quite right to love
his faults as well

Except that he left us
with no time to say goodbye
And I'm now scratching my head
over the question of correct selection
Selection of the fittest form of life
genuine values in art
and actions in politics
the best forest the right riverbed
comfortable shoes and uncomfortable friends
or even dishes from a menu

And there's selection and selection
Surely it matters
who is selecting whom or what    And why
For what purpose    Under what circumstances
And on what grounds

Racial characteristics appeal or origin
will not presumably be the right criteria
any more than pretended
zeal in faith

Moreover there are certain things on earth
that one simply can't choose for oneself
(among them for instance are
parents native land and one's own genes)
And others covered by the ancient saying
that He that chooses
often loses

And yet out of three million Czechoslovak women
of what is called child-bearing age
I've chosen you
It took me a long time
And it took us a good deal longer still
jointly to choose
our wedding menu

We had a skirmish
over entrée soup aperitif
The laws of selection however are inflexible
The stronger one wins
And so you won

The Balt-Orient Express is just getting its breath back
under the vault of Brno station
And so am I between two great battles
Petrov is vanishing in the mist
And Špilberk is not yet visible

I make a note in my diary
that 15th February 1980 was a foggy day
with rain
I'm feeling like a victor
because at this time tomorrow
you'll be my own second wife
Even though it's quite possible
that this selection business was
the other way round

*Jaroslav Čejka translated by Ewald Osers*

# Designer Kidz Song

Goodbye faerie, cripple and yid –
Get a clone of your own Designer Kid
Kids no doting mother ever had,
Created by Selecta-Dad.
We're the market leaders in the race
To privatise the human face.
We've cracked the code of the chromosome
With a logo guaranteed on every bone!

Goodbye guesswork – Fanny or Dick?–
Bio-tech select the sex you pick.
Mix'n'match for colour and size,
For the ears of a prince or Einstein's eyes.
And if you've got a gene the future needs
Selecta-Dad 'll bank your seeds.
And if you've gotta gene that didn't oughta be
There's a free vasec- or hysterec- tomy.

Goodbye curse of bloody motherhood
Those labour pains are gone for good.
There's no danger, there's no fuss
With a new designer uterus.
Designer girls don't reproduce,
They're just for recreational use.
Selected for servility
With a lifetime money-back guarantee!

Goodbye pain and bothersome bugs,
Hello to a body with built-in drugs!
Hybrid flesh that 'll never go bad,
Created by Selecta-Dad.
Selecta-Dad comes to you from
The fathers of the Atom Bomb,
 Chernobyl, genocide,
Asbestos and thalidomide.

Oh! Goodbye world gone horribly wrong,
The march of progress marches on,
Delivering strength, delivering joy,
In a blond and blue-eyed bargain boy.
And if that infant later on
says "Foster Daddy, where did I come from?"
Say "A womb in a room in a white-walled lab,
The brain child of Selecta-Dad."

Goodbye conscience, chicken and cow,
Getta burger without cruelty now.
Beefsteak culture growing on a shelf,
The meat that 'll cook and eat itself!
There's a Big-Mac logo kids'll love
On the wings of the new designer-dove;
A factory-forest and so much more –
You've no idea what shit's in store!

Goodbye Ancient Mystery,
The call of the wild is history.
We'll weed out indigenous sperm
With the aid of a smart Designer-Germ.
Select the hot-shots that we need
For a cleaner, leaner, meaner breed;
A gene-elite in a righteous war,
To waste whatever was on earth before.

Goodbye evolutionary tree –
We have beavered away in secrecy,
Laboured and brought forth a Son:
The Immortal, Polymeris-ed One,
With perfect skin, perfect skill,
To do His Father's perfect will
On a world forever in His control,
A playground for Selected Souls.

Goodbye gullible homo-sapiens
You believed your deceivers were your friends.
Trusted us to change your lot
'Til you lost the only lot you'd got.
Selecta-Dad would like to thank
The cream of the cream in the donor bank.
And on your mother's grave we swear:

"Though we have left you in the lurch
We shall not cease from our research
Til we can resurrect the toss
Of the Fuehrer whose idea it was!"

Theo Simon, *Seize the Day*

# Of Weaning and Desire

Milk is the matrix of this culture
I keep it alive in a hand-thrown cup
painted with a woman's face
her hair an uncontrolled radiance

    She was the woman who squeezed from her breast
    drops of her last milk
    before her last child was weaned
    stirred them into a bowl of fresh cow's milk
    let it sit all night beside the stove
    humming and warming to a lyric thickness

    Bowl    cup    breast    song
    a spoon at a time
    the child is nourished
    by the bowl of cultured milk
    she calls it *viili*
    never questions its continual fullness
    as the infant accepts its mother's breast

    The child grows to womanhood.
    On her marriage morning
    her mother unplaits and brushes her hair,
    blesses her with three gifts:
    a wedding rug in colours of spring,
    a hand-thrown bowl glazed in sky,
    a square of cheesecloth
    dipped in *viili*, dried in the sun

    Take these with you, my daughter.
    The rug will warm your bed,
    give you children.
    The bowl is for milk,
    soak the cheesecloth in it
    and the *viili* will be reborn

I am the one who must keep this alive –
it has been carried through centuries across borders,
even now the women conspire and hide
the dried cheesecloth in envelopes
undetectable by airport X-rays

My breasts are dry, my children grown.
I live without custom, eat what I need,
cut my hair short. I keep this alive
not for my daughter, who does not know its taste,
but for my mother, for all the Marias,
their ancient desire enclosed in a cup

*Nancy Mattson*

# Impure Science

with impatient shuttle
we pleach unknown fibres
into the warp and weft of life
and hold our woven breath

*Stephen Hancock*

# Amoral Maize

So now the very threads of life are ours
Painstakingly laid bare they tantalize;
Their subtle patterns spell temptation –
Enough to make us all Prometheus.
But the fiercest fires burn in accountants' eyes.

Captains of industry
Dazzled by this fervid light
Lose sight of trusty lode-star's dimmer certainties
And helm their businesses, dismissive of disaster,
Towards the fastest buck.

*Don Warman*

# Spliced

Quiet under the tree a snowdrop sleeping
virgin of drifts, not the kind to marry
an ear of wheat - old as Pharoah's granary
inbred fruit of the plains, born to be eaten –

No Christian coupling this, church of science
Monsanto priests, dressed in white, endeavour
– neater than Adam's rib and twice as clever –
a delicate experimental splice

A mating most fecund, sowing defiled oats
like dragons' teeth, alien corn in the guts
every bit we eat a breaking down
till we surrender, we are not immune

and tricky new viruses appear, weird
as a snowdrop's heart inside a cornstalk's ear

Hylda Sims

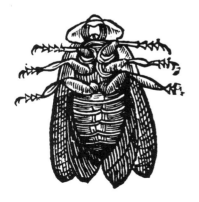

23

# A Word Puzzle

Lewis Carroll in 1879 invented a puzzle named Doublets, in which two words of equal length are linked together by interposing other words, each differing from the previous word by one letter only, until the transformation is accomplished.

Lewis Carroll thought this puzzle "very soothing: what doctors call 'an alterative', i.e. if you happen to have a headache, it will charm it away: but if you haven't one, it will probably give you one..."

"The rules of the puzzle are simple enough...The letters must not be interchanged among themselves, but each must keep to its own place....It is perhaps needless to state that it is *de rigueur* that the links should be English words, such as might be used in good society."

He gave as example the word 'head' which he changed into 'tail' in four links:

**HEAD**
HEAL
TEAL
TELL
TALL
**TAIL**

Who would have thought that such a charming brain-teaser could have implications for our present day? When Lewis Carroll changed BIRD into FISH in four links, the game was no more than a mental exercise.

Here is how a COW may grow MAD (my own version, there could be others).

**COW**
COD
CAD
**MAD**

The next quotation is from my much-thumbed copy of *The Magic of Lewis Carroll* (edited by John Fisher, 1973) : "John Maynard Smith, exploring the process by which one species evolves from another in an essay entitled 'The Limitations of Molecular Evolution' from *The Scientist Speculates: an anthology of partly baked ideas,* uses Lewis Carroll's 'doublets' to extend the analogy between the messages in words and the genetic instructions in chromosomes. He instances the change of WORD to GENE in three links:

**WORD**
WORE
GORE
GONE
**GENE** "

John Fisher commented:
"One has only to think of the helical DNA molecule as a word, with each successive change in that structure, the basis of evolution, as a change in letter, to realise that when Carroll evolved MAN from APE he was closer to reality than he could have dreamed."

**APE**
ARE
ERE
ERR
EAR
MAR
**MAN**

*John Rety*

# Two Fantasies

## 1: The Past

### Rose Buds

Correct in the breeding arithmetic,
Roses emerge from the bud's origami
Like a born virtuoso,
With every crease that might betray
Origin in wilderness
Smoothed over, and the paper cleansed.

Given the greatest sun,
They must assert the vital promise
As yet unsaid, but written in their heritage,
To flame like a sunset even brighter than
The day before, with glory
To the ancestral hue.

Asleep they discover that colour
for themselves, dreaming of when
Their flower grew more beautiful
And bold than other weeds,
Soliciting for carriers
To pass on the pollen.

Before their bloodline was selected
And spliced into one hybrid vision,
Like a painting reworked
Until the richness of the colour
And perfected light and shade
Made the image real and raised it from the page.

In the artificial warmth
The rose buds dangle like dark green
Chrysalids, clinging to their stalk,
Unfolding as if inflated by
The pressure to forget
Everything they'd known unborn.

# 2: The Far Future

## Meta-Biology

We were taught from school to deal with future shock,
To quote yesterday's news like history,
And rush with open arms towards the next
New miracle,
But always ready to deal with
That strange fear of not quite knowing
What we would become, or what to do, when
The Daemons, when they spoke, unleashed
Their bright new vision to redevelop us
Every generation.

Waiting at the bottom of the ocean
For cast off news, they monitor
Our prosperity and health,
Sometimes gauge the failures when
They think too far ahead, or intensify
The conditioning to compensate.
While in our every living cell wait
The genetic masons, benignly fixing flaws,
Until a blueprint is relayed to them.
They re-craft our DNA.

Philosophers agree, this is the end
Of evolution.
No longer the incidental egg for passing on
Family traits, merely for survival,
Freed from the tyranny of mutation and selection.
No more the coded legacy we used to carry
Like a manual, as if we could not be trusted
To remember who we are.

Projections show no more
Of nature's accidental heroes will exist
Next year. The automatic masons pick them out.
One Orchid was preserved, one Bee,
One Hummingbird,
But fewer people go to see them.
I pressed my ear to the ground, but all I could hear
Was the Earth growl impotently back,
Like a stomach whose last meal had been creation.

*Matt Ford*

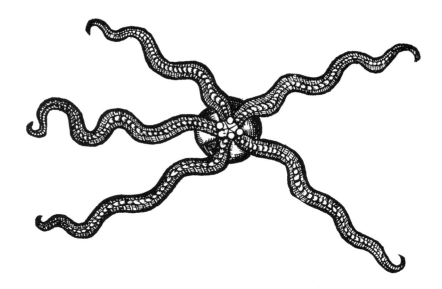

# Perseus in Retrospect

He came in swaggering, full of bright ideas
about the use of fire. How it would harden,
and ore be hammered out, tempered to the core
as steel. How he would hone a blade, hack

seasoned ash with his adze, forming a shaft;
and, crafting a winged scoop he called a share,
would wade into the soil, the heavy tip tearing
into the sun-baked surface, turning the earth.

How he would harness the horse, cajole him to pull
the assembly, furrow the ground as needed for seeding;
thrash the harvest, garnered by her, his flails
raining the chaff; afterwards grinding the grain

for flour; yeasting and kneading the dough; baking it
on stones heated by fire. Full of himself
and sensing his power, her glowering silence stilled him,
filled him with foreboding; and she began:

I suppose I foresaw what Solomon said: Black,
but comely; a garden enclosed is my sister, my spouse;
her lips drop as the honey-comb; the scent of Lebanon
fills, etcetera; my breasts appear like pomegranates.

She came snake-maned and overlaid
with instinct. Bleeding beyond her boundaries, she got him
with her eyes. He asked if Agent Orange and a spot
of acid rain were plain to prescience. Petrified

at what he saw ensouled, and shielding his eye,
he shrank from her real beauty. His foresight waned,
and, wielding all his weaponry, he slew her; blaming
nature, and naming his monstrous act, duty.

David Kuhrt

# Magic Roundabout

Inside these cells
   ancestors ring tiny bells
      reminders of earth-life before.
        Do we trek forward

or back? Ask Cleopatra –
   torpid fortune-teller
      egg-yellow palms –
        she hazards our history

from thin amoebic trails.
   We dice with chance to meet
      in the gamblers' arcade,
        your face a throwback

of the colonel who tricked
   two tank-brigades
      and before who built
        the Trojan horse.

Our proteins fuse then separate –
   shy strands of DNA
      like clog-heeled teenagers
        at their first school dance.

For inside each cell
   the virus rings tiny bells
      reminders of life lost before
        do we trek forward?

Danielle Hope

# The New Magic

Take the i from genie
Reveal the gene
Whose awesome powers
We tyros would command.
But what magician of yore
Would ever dare
To uncork a magic bottle
Knowing its genie was blind.

Don Warman

# Dear Dawkins...

## for James Everard

Dear Dawkins, disciple of Darwin,
though you allege "We're privileged to be,
in one sense, lumps of matter", it's this,
not molecules, which gets me laughing.

If melancholy logic is opposed to humour
and genes cause both, the cryptic river
contradicts itself. I stand aside
to argue, thinking: What a bloomer!

Your universe is like liberal democracy:
as lumps we're levelled down. A steady state
is always uniform. If matter is,
explain: how do we get complexity?

Your simple formula's a cop-out
to conformity. It masquerades as fact
a point of view which hides philosophy,
for judgement's what this is about.

No entity is known to science
which thinking has not first recorded.
Does matter cross your mind? If I differ
is it this, or thought gives guidance?

The eloquent argument you put disputing it
is inimical to facts. Show me the mechanism
which moves a gene to lie; how selfishness
upsets the applecart and speaks the truth.

Don't deny your existence. The blind force
is yours, not evolution's. Did nature
need your gerrymandering to bring
a material world to birth in thought –

in which the parts know very well
the whole won't work unless assent
to common wealth, justice, equitable
rewards, defines selfishness as hell.

This hell is never nature's. She spawns
diversity and abandon's blind alleys
Yet, ill-matched with circumstance,
you rant against the evidence: spirit's a form

which moved across the stage of change
to bring forward the kind of thing we are.
Existence in you is aware of Dawkins, not
of matter only. You think in a maze –

the bit you feel, and are, is Ariadne.
Abstract intellect is a Minotaur which winds
to its constructed cave the more she calls: Dawkins,
let's get laid before the monster has me.

The martial gene is your invention, mate.
No upset applecart can lurch ahead
itself to climactic catastrophe. If we
like the redundant dodo do, ours isn't fate.

If, like the dodo, you've lost the nerve
to exist, don't speak for me. It's you
who abdicates. Genes yield the Crown
to those who think: it's nature I serve.

Your problem here's complexity:
no blue-print yet exists for this.
The highest common factor's not in facts.
It's thinking which establishes the key.

The genes were never selfish: sinking differences
They fought so you and I might survive
and see how thought is free to sink the ship.
Your theories verge on brinkmanship.

Dear Dawkins, the blind watchmaker
fills a void you ought to occupy.
The selfish gene's a cancer in a vacuum.
That's a thing which nature never tolerates.

                                                    David Kuhrt

# Ramifications

Such a paradox it does not live,
That which plans our lives.
Those tight skeined molecules
Ambassadors for evolution
Embassied one hundred billion times
To guard our bodies' regimented march to death.

And do not think that at our demise,
Embassies sundered,
Ambassadors scattered
Carrying their instructions,
These messages will drop to oblivion.

Oh, by the million they will vanish,
But in their very number lies a perpetuity.
And in the corner of some foreign field
Worms may ingest an archive
That was a human consciousness.

*Don Warman*

# Food'n'Health'n'Hope

Those Polar Bears now – who really cares now?
They're breeding gender-bending babies, who won't be breeding none
Cos PCBs, yeah, are in the seas, yeah
We like to think that there's a little piece of us in everyone!

> Cos we're Monsanto – that's right Monsanto
> We're turning Satan into Santa, by giving kiddies cancer
> Coming through now, we're changing you now,
> The Mother-Nature Terminators of Food'n'Health'n'Hope

That DDT ban - don't lay it on me man!
Cos we had all these creepie-crawlies fallin' on the food we grew,
Was a revolution-ary solution
It's just a shame that what we sprayed on made the turnips toxic too!

Let me remind yer 'bout Indochina,
Then commie dominoes were fallin' so we sprayed 'em into hell,
Give peasant farmers Orange pyjamas –
We made their jungle cover wither, then we withered them as well!

> Cos we're Monsanto – that's right Monsanto
> We're turning Satan into Santa, by giving kiddies cancer
> Coming through now, we're changing you now,
> The Mother-Nature Terminators of Food'n'Health'n'Hope

It's not our fault there's chem-ical warfare
But if there's dollars in dioxin, it's our duty to supply
That rain of poison they washed our boys in,
A cancer-agent from the C.I. – Hey! – I cannot tell a lie

From Pentagon came that drug Aspartame,
Our Pepsi-Cola with no calories was every kiddie's treat.
When there were rumours it gave 'em tumours
Somebody falsified the data, and we called it NutraSweet

And you get more juice now from a dairy moo-cow,
Monsanto's daily dose of hormone's, them udders gonna swell!
– Don't blame the cream though, if you're in chemo,
There may be BST mastectomies, but nobody can tell!

    Cos we're Monsanto - that's right Monsanto
    We're turning Satan into Santa, by giving kiddies cancer
    Coming through now, we're changing you now,
    The Mother-Nature Terminators of Food'n'Health'n'Hope

Robert Shapiro, well, he's our Hero!
He's on a mission with a vision of 'Sustainability'
Which means we're goin' to keep on growin'
Till we're the biggest corporation in the 21st Century!

Seeing no future for the big polluters
He span an 'eco-friendly' line in redesigning DNA,
Genetic eyes on that far horizon
Where every thing alive is privatised and every seed'll pay.

We've got the soya, we got the lawyers,
The politicians in our pockets all the way to President!
The press and T.V. to guarantee the
Co-operation of your nation in our new experiment.

You did not choose it, but you'll have to use it:
We'll get our 'Roundup-Ready' fingerprint in every pie you eat,
With every patent, be a bit more blatant,
Till our corporation's domination of your globe'll be complete!

Mister Monsanto! Monster Mutanto!
We're turning Satan into Santa – Give Everybody Cancer!
Coming through now, we're changing you now,
The Mother-Nature Terminators,
Hell-On-Earth Creators,
Gene-Manipulators,
Bio-tech Dictators.
The Future's gonna hate us...

Food'n'Health'n'Hope!

*Seize the Day*

# Now I Know

Now I know how nature is
like putty in my hands, she's mine
to deflower; a bride wizened
until the thinned frame gives.

Although it may be best to ask:
Is nature not aware her hands
are mine? If so, she planned,
foresaw the trick of consciousness

which says: If time exists,
no chromosome could know the trend
would end with homo sapiens.
Matter mirrors itself, I think.

Such distance as there is
from start to finish is subjective.
The particles which underpin the seed
foresaw the bloom. It's us that wears it.

David Kuhrt

# There's Something in the Air

            though it's a clear day
paler than the wind, stranger than the sea
something moving there though you can't hear it
carried on the breeze, falling free

something in the rain, though it's a fine rain
gauze across the sky, brushstrokes on the skin
something septic there though you can't find it
captured by the mist but falling free

something in the land though it's a good land
darker than the earth, deeper than a tree
something sleeping there beneath the plough's hand
growing in the crops and rising free

something in the plants though they are good plants
each silent folded leaf as perfect as a dream
something waiting there inside the silence
ready for the lambs to take their feast

something in the air chill as December
something in the rain dry as any bone
something in the land my love remember
fell as any crime, blind as any stone


Hylda Sims

# Brecht

Brecht, where are you when we need you now?
They're forcing things down our throats.
Genetically modified mad cows,
germs without antidotes.
And our voices are stilled with prosperity
or hopelessness, or both.
Brecht, when that Wall came down in Germany
we breathed a sigh. At last
we thought,the whole world's free!
But all that was free were the crooks. And I am past
the stage of euphemism. Where
are your daughters, where your sons, to blast
away the dust-motes of despair?
To sing the true note, with genius and gall
that free isn't free till it's fair?
Why didn't we see the wall behind the Wall?

Leah Fritz

# Contributors